You're One Cool Cat

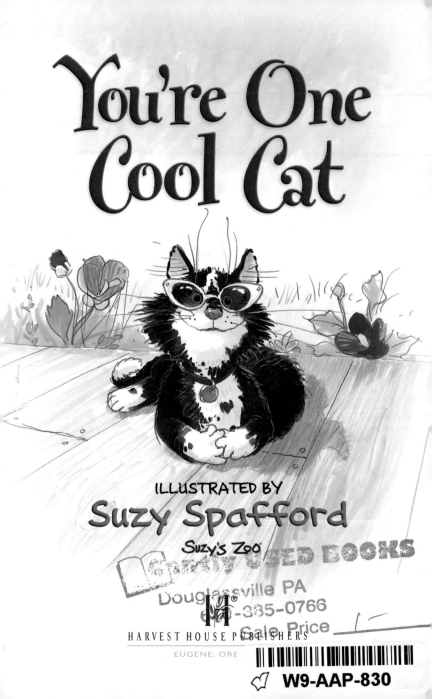

ILLUSTRATED BY

Suzy Spafford

Suzy's Zoo®

HARVEST HOUSE PUBLISHERS

EUGENE, ORE

You're One Cool Cat

Text Copyright © 2004 by Harvest House Publishers
Eugene, Oregon 97402

ISBN 0-7369-1416-1

Original artwork © Suzy Spafford. Wags and Whiskers™ is a trademark
of Suzy's Zoo, A California Corporation.

Design and production by Garborg Design Works, Minneapolis,
Minnesota

Printed in China.

04 05 06 07 08 09 10 11 12 13 / LP / 10 9 8 7 6 5 4 3 2 1

To:

Claire

From:

Grandma

You're One Cool Cat!

While others try to figure you out...you know just who you are.

I don't understand,
but the occasional mystery,
the otherness of cats,
is part of their charm.

BARBARA HOLLAND

You are confident, mysterious, and so very cool.

To be what we are, and to become what we are capable of becoming, is the only end of life.

ROBERT LOUIS STEVENSON

I awoke this morning
   for my friends,

Let us, then, be what we are, and speak
what we think, and in all things keep
ourselves loyal to truth and the sacred
professions of friendship.

HENRY WADSWORTH LONGFELLOW

with devout thanksgiving
the old and the new.

RALPH WALDO EMERSON

You consider naps and baths to be a fabulous use of an afternoon.

There are people who reshape the world by force or argument, but the cat just lies there, dozing, and the world quietly reshapes itself to suit his comfort and convenience.

ALLEN AND IVY DODD

By sharing in your joy of the simple things,
I appreciate life more.

In the sweetness of friendship let there

Being with my best friends
was more refreshing than a
massage and a hot bath and long
summer's nap all together.

BECKY FREEMAN

You have let me experience the joys
of life and the exquisite pleasures
of your own eternal presence.

THE BOOK OF PSALMS

be laughter, and sharing of pleasures.

KAHLIL GIBRAN

*Friendship is a strong and habitual
inclination in two persons to promote
the good and happiness of one another.*

EUSTACE BUDGELL

You're independent and still like to have me around.

The cat may disappear on its own errands, but sooner or later, it returns once again for a little while, to greet us with its own type of love. Independent as they are, cats find more than pleasure in our company.

LLOYD ALEXANDER

I feel special because you make time
to hear my thoughts. To ask my opinions.
To just be with me…little ol' me.

Life is to be fortified by
many friendships. To love
and to be loved is the greatest
happiness of existence.

SYDNEY SMITH

Only solitary men know the full joys of friendship. Others have their family; but to a solitary and an exile his friends are everything.

WARREN G. HARDING

Perhaps the most delightful friendships are those in which there is much agreement, much disputation, and yet more personal liking.

GEORGE ELIOT

Count your age with

friends but not with years.

ANONYMOUS

You accept me for me.

What greater gift than the love of a cat?

CHARLES DICKENS

When I am with you, I don't have to pretend to be someone I'm not. If I ever try, you are quick to bring me back to myself.

A friend is one who knows

A true friend is someone who thinks that you are a good egg even though he knows that you are slightly cracked.

BERNARD MELTZER

The most basic and powerful way to connect to another person is to listen. Just listen. Perhaps the most important thing we ever give each other is our attention...A loving silence often has far more power to heal and to connect than the most well-intentioned words.

RACHEL NAOMI REMEN

us, but loves us anyway.

JEROME CUMMINGS

There can be no friendship
where there is no freedom.

WILLIAM PENN

You know where all the great places are.

If a dog jumps into your lap it is
because he is fond of you;
but if a cat does the same thing
it is because your lap is warmer.

ALFRED NORTH WHITEHEAD

*How did you ever find that perfect café with the
view? Your "ideal location" radar is finely tuned.
I'd follow you anywhere.*

Every man has within himself a
continent of undiscovered character.
Happy is he who proves the
Columbus of his soul.

GOETHE

Good company in a journey

We are all travelers in the
wilderness of this world,
and the best we can find in
our travels is an honest friend.

ROBERT LOUIS STEVENSON

makes the way seem shorter.

IZAAK WALTON

You're unique.

Way down deep, we're all
motivated by the same urges.
Cats have the courage
to live by them.

JIM DAVIS

Stylish. Graceful. Poised.
All that and a bit of craziness.
Your extraordinary mix of traits adds up
to the definition of "friend."

A friend may well be reckoned the

When we seek to discover the best
in others, we somehow bring out
the best in ourselves.

WILLIAM ARTHUR WARD

masterpiece of nature.

RALPH WALDO EMERSON

If a man does not
keep pace with his
companions, perhaps
it is because he hears
a different drummer.
Let him step to
the music which
he hears, however
measured or far away.

HENRY DAVID THOREAU

We can never replace a friend.
When a man is fortunate
enough to have several, he finds
they are all different. No one
has a double in friendship.

FRIEDRICH SCHILLER

29

You tell me just what I need to hear... without speaking a word.

A meow massages the heart.

STUART McMILLAN

In the blink of an eye, a shrug of a shoulder, or a flash of a smile, you say it all.

If instead of a gem, or even a flower, we should cast the gift of a loving thought into the heart of a friend, that would be giving as the angels give.

GEORGE MACDONALD

True friendship comes when silence

Every man, however wise,
needs the advice
of some sagacious friend
in the affairs of life.

PLAUTUS

between two people is comfortable.

DAVE TYSON GENTRY

A pleasant possession is

useless without a friend.
SENECA

You don't notice my shortcomings.

As anyone who has ever been around a cat for any length of time well knows cats have enormous patience with the limitations of the human kind.

CLEVELAND AMORY

Well, at least you never mention my failings…and that's even nicer!

I always felt that the great high privilege, relief and comfort of friendship was that one had to explain nothing.

KATHERINE MANSFIELD

If we all told what we know of one another, there would not be four friends in the world.

BLAISE PASCAL

Love is blind, but

Your friend is the man
who knows all about you,
and still likes you.

ELBERT HUBBARD

friendship closes its eyes.

AUTHOR UNKNOWN

Your curious nature makes life an adventure.

An ordinary kitten will
ask more questions than
any five-year-old boy.

CARL VAN VECHTEN

I can never drag my heels when you are
around. You whisk me off on another
escapade…and I have the best moments,
best memories, best laughs of my life.

Curiosity is one of the permanent and

A true friend unbosoms freely,
advises justly, assists readily,
adventures boldly, takes all
patiently, defends courageously,
and continues a friend unchangeably.

WILLIAM PENN

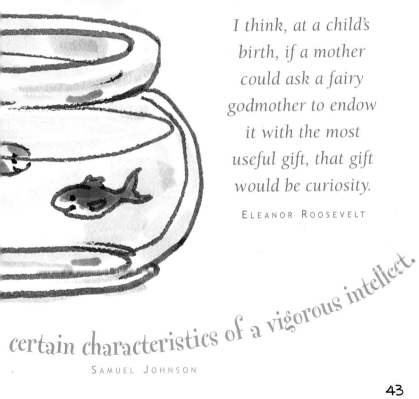

*I think, at a child's
birth, if a mother
could ask a fairy
godmother to endow
it with the most
useful gift, that gift
would be curiosity.*

ELEANOR ROOSEVELT

certain characteristics of a vigorous intellect.

SAMUEL JOHNSON

I can tell you absolutely anything.

Cats are designated friends.

NORMAN CORWIN

*You are my confidant, my safe place,
my shoulder to lean on.*

We need people in our lives
with whom we can be as open as
possible. To have real conversation
with people may seem like such
a simple, obvious suggestion,
but it involves courage and risk.

DR. THOMAS MOORE

Yes, I shall see him, not as a stranger,

Oh, the comfort, the inexpressible comfort
of feeling safe with a person having neither
to weigh thoughts nor measure words,
but pouring them all right out, just as they are,
chaff and grain together; certain that
a faithful hand will take and sift them,
keep what is worth keeping, and then with
the breath of kindness blow the rest away.

DINAH MARIA MULOCK CRAIK

but as a friend! What a glorious hope!

THE BOOK OF JOB

Plant a seed of friendship;
reap a bouquet of happiness.

Lois L. Kaufman